Dream
Big
Love
Bigger

Dive
Deep
Into
Life's
Ocean

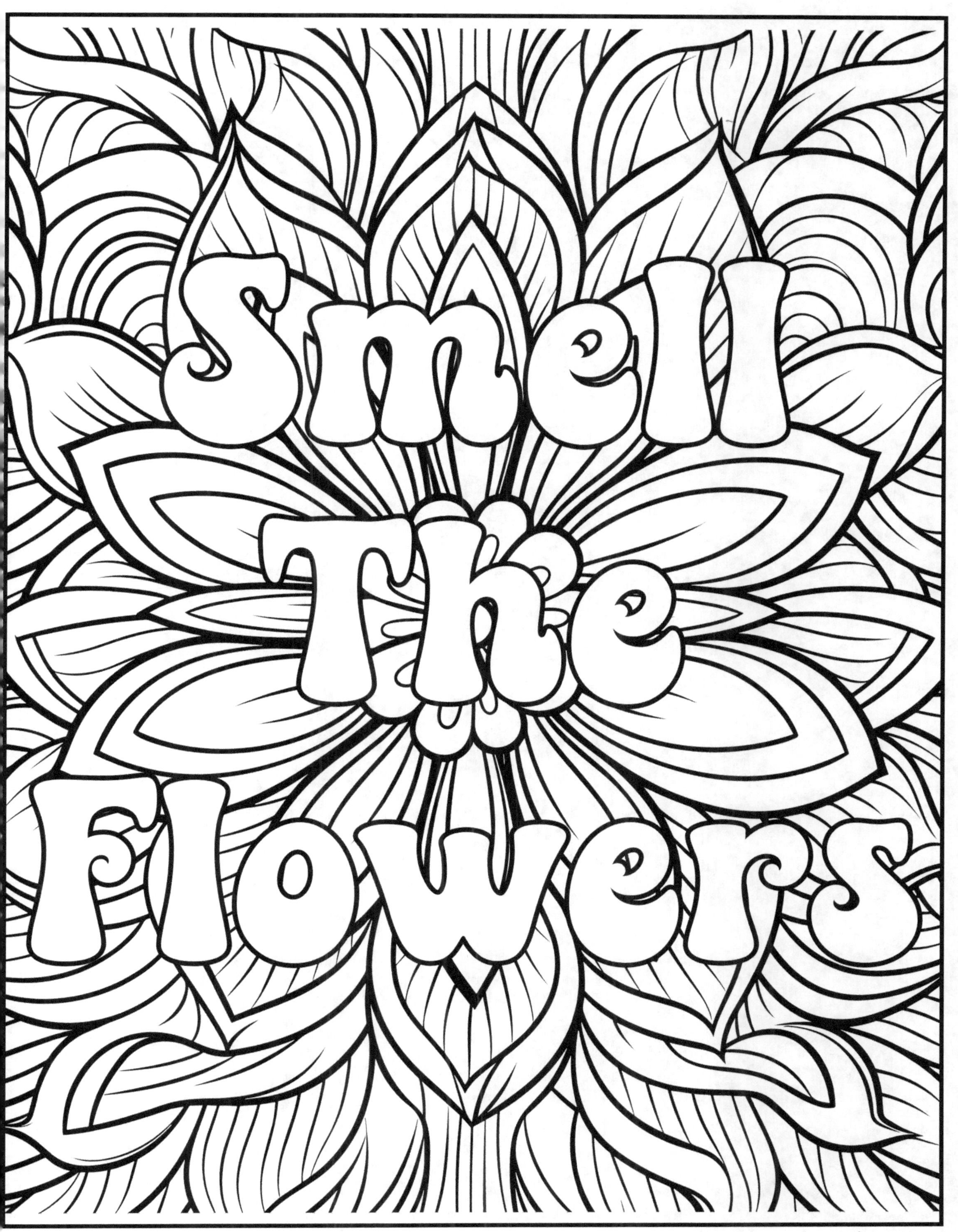

Smell
The
Flowers

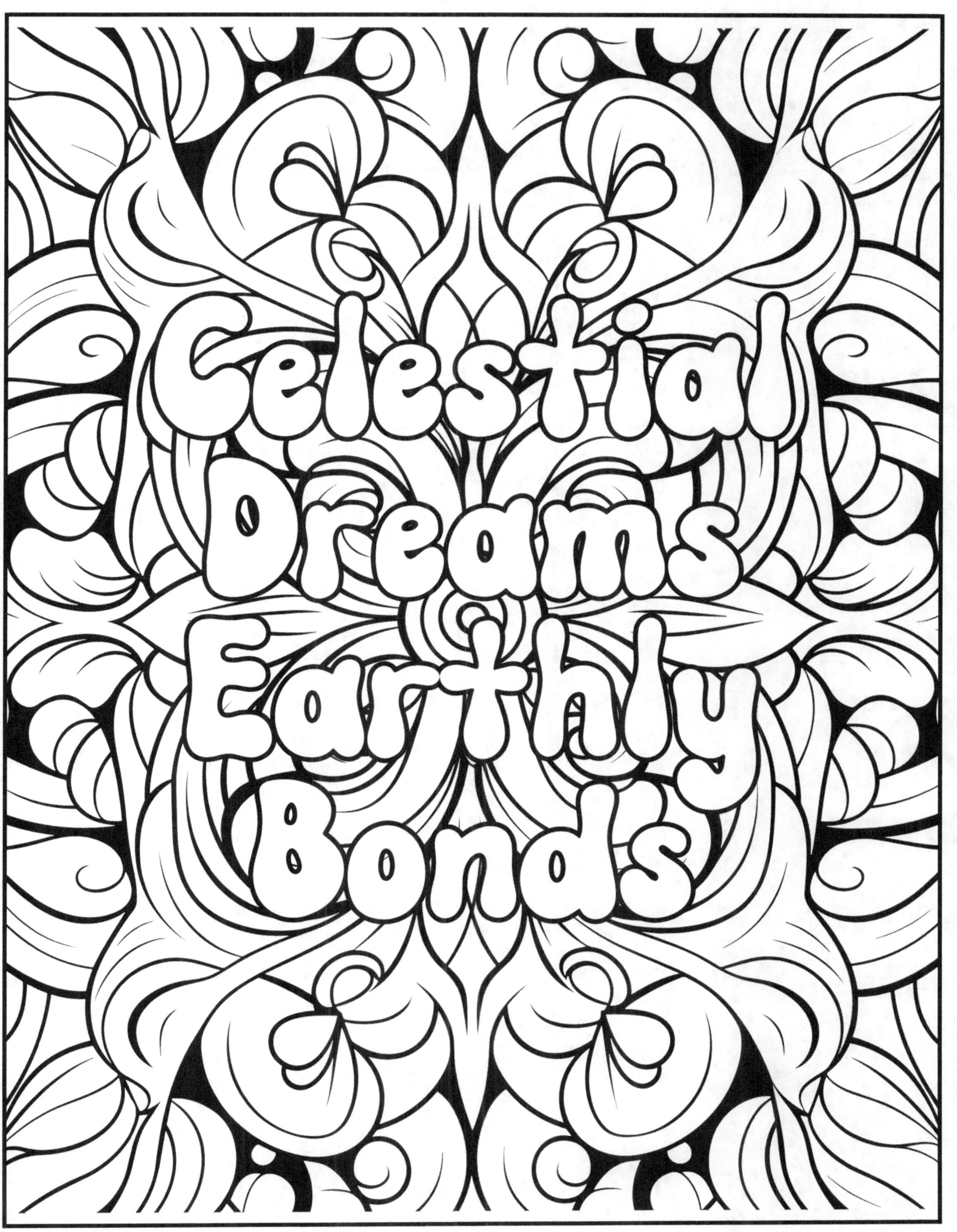
Celestial Dreams Earthly Bonds

Love
And
Let
Love

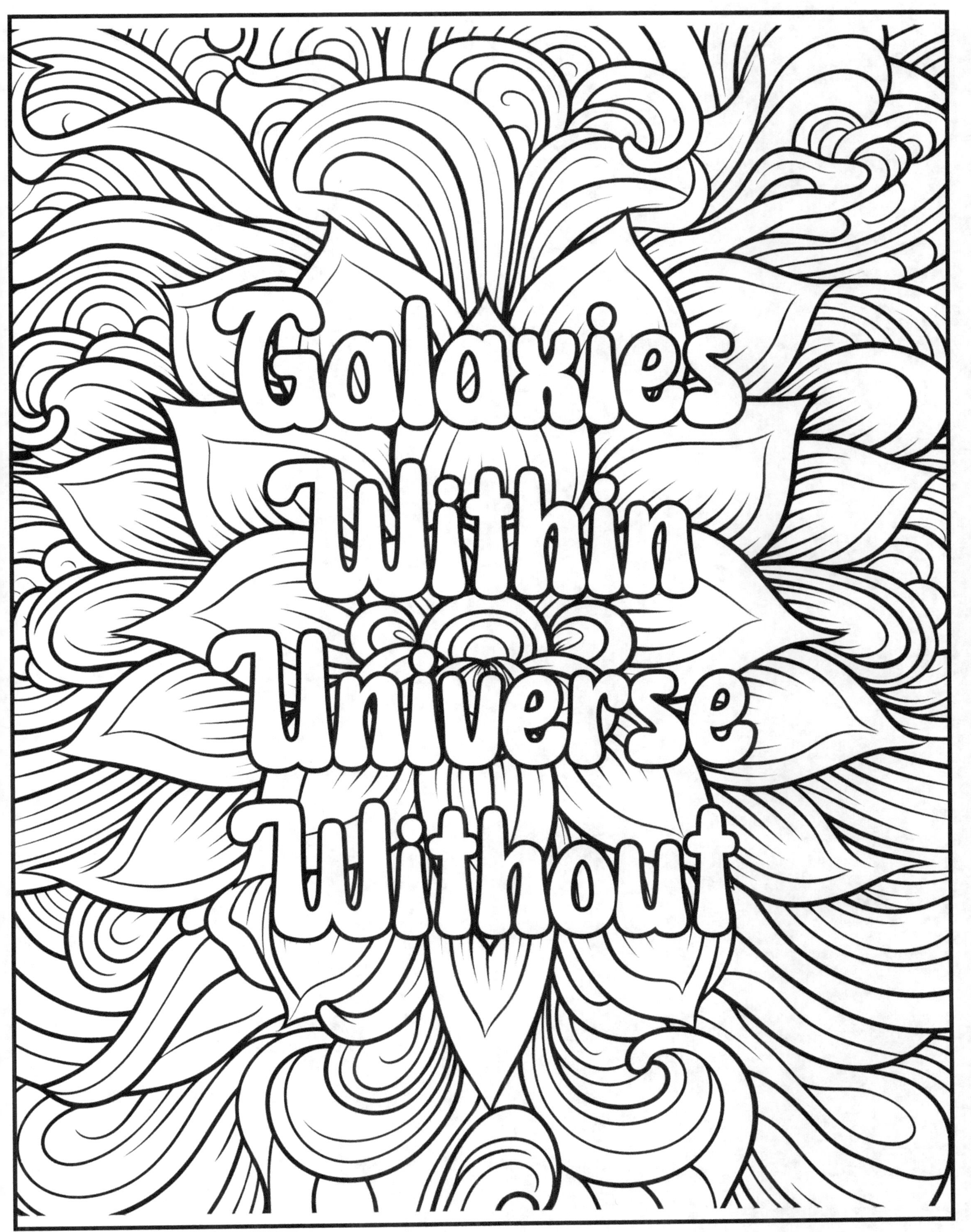

Galaxies
Within
Universe
Without

Seek
Love
Spread
peace

VIBES
OF
PEACE
EXPAND

Love's
Eternal
Flame
Burns

Love
More
Worry
Less

Love's
Journey
Life's
Rhythm

Dreams
Painted
In
Peace

Let's
Wander
Where
Wifi
Is
Weak

Be
The
Energy
You
Seek

Cosmic
Love
Earthly
Joy

Lost
In
The
Right
Direction

Every
Leaf
Tells
A
Story

By
Stars
We
Navigate

Life
Is
A
Wild
Ride

Love
Vibes
Spirits
Soar

Spread
Kind
Vibes

Hippie
Soul
Gypsy
Heart

Hues
Of
Love
In
Every
Dawn

Eclipsing
Doubts
Embracing
Dreams

By
Moonlight
We
Thrive

Hope
Anchors
The
Soul

Earth
Child
Star
Born

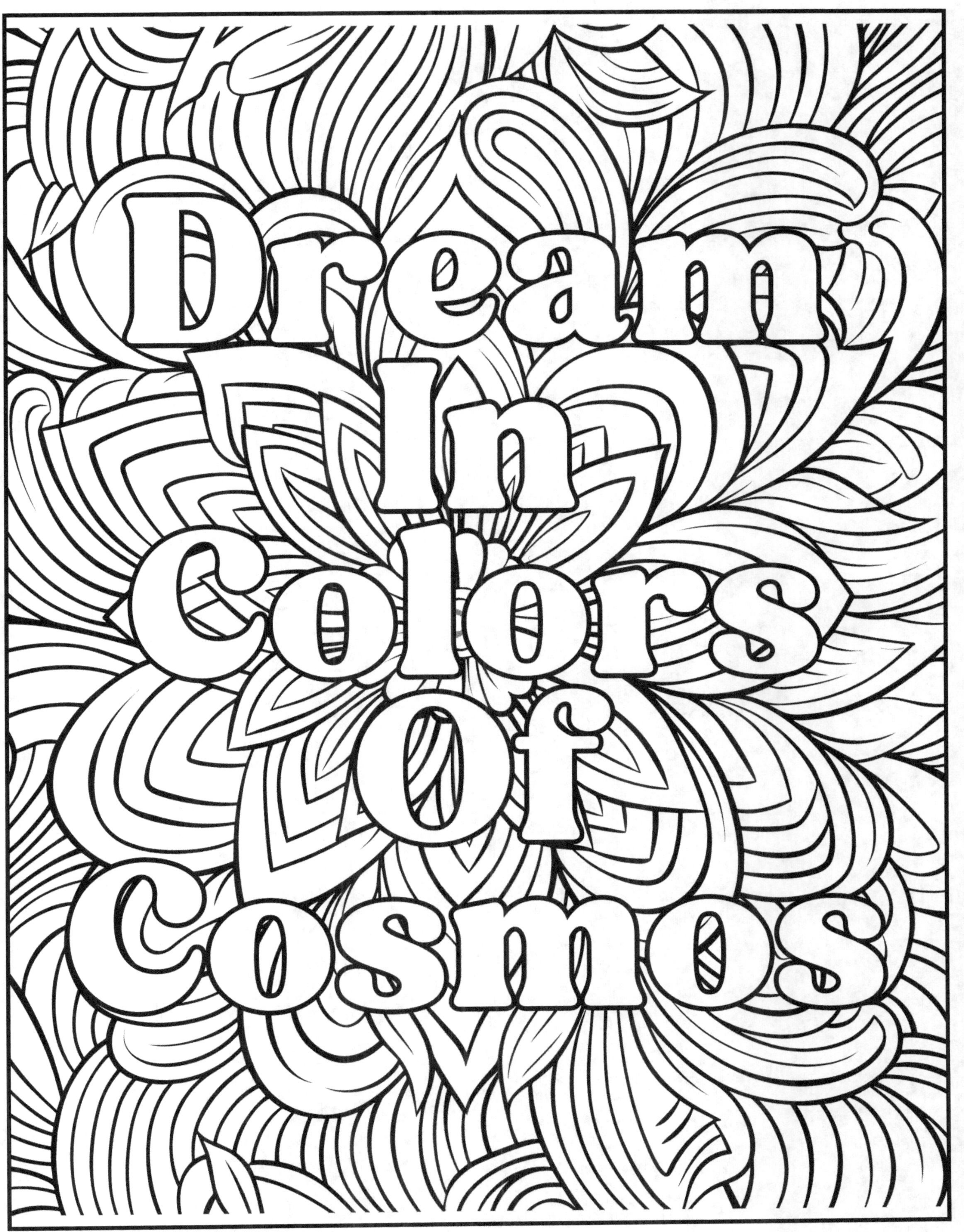

Dreams In Colors Of Cosmos

Music
Heals
The
Soul

SUNSHINE
MIXED
WITH
COURAGE

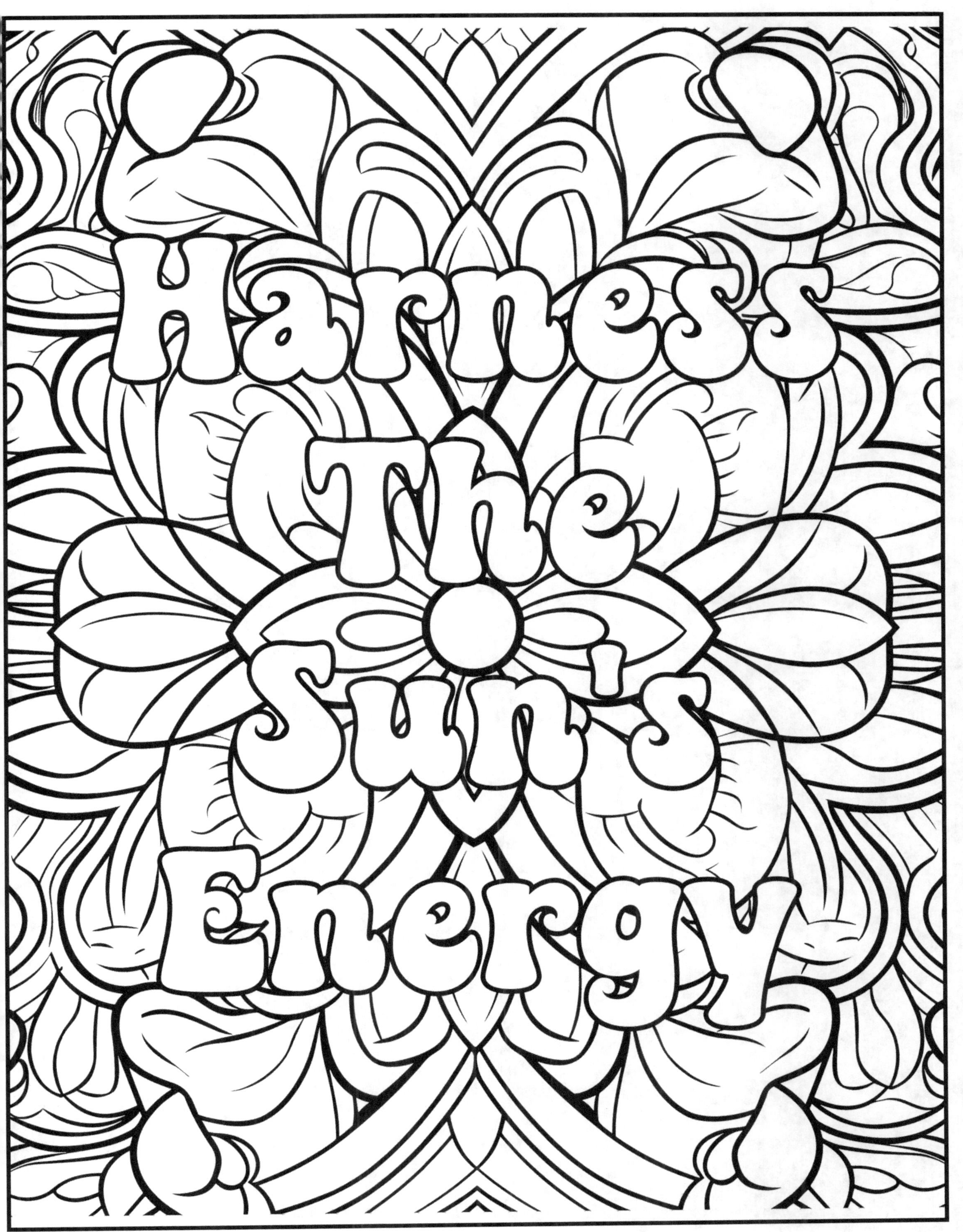

Harness
The
Sun's
Energy

Peace Signs And Tie Dye

Dance
With
The
Wind

Flower
Power
Forever

HIPPIE
HEARTS
UNITE

From
Cosmic
Chaos
Comes
Clarity

Soul
Full
Of
Sunshine

Voyaging
Via
Heart's
Vision

Lost
In
Love's
Labyrinth

Love
Is
The
Answer

Chase
Dreams
Not
Things

Stardust
Soul
Seeking
Serenity

LIFE'S
DANCE
LOVE'S
RHYTHM

Carve
Dreams
Not
Fears